KV-193-509

My Life Adventures

PETER DAZ

authorHOUSE®

AuthorHouse™ UK
1663 Liberty Drive
Bloomington, IN 47403 USA
www.authorhouse.co.uk
Phone: UK TFN: 0800 0148641 (Toll Free inside the UK)
*   UK Local: (02) 0369 56322 (+44 20 3695 6322 from outside the UK)*

© 2021 Peter Daz. All rights reserved.

No part of this book may be reproduced, stored in a retrieval system, or transmitted by any means without the written permission of the author.

Published by AuthorHouse 10/14/2021

ISBN: 978-1-6655-9404-2 (sc)
ISBN: 978-1-6655-9403-5 (hc)
ISBN: 978-1-6655-9405-9 (e)

Print information available on the last page.

Any people depicted in stock imagery provided by Getty Images are models, and such images are being used for illustrative purposes only.
Certain stock imagery © Getty Images.

This book is printed on acid-free paper.

Because of the dynamic nature of the Internet, any web addresses or links contained in this book may have changed since publication and may no longer be valid. The views expressed in this work are solely those of the author and do not necessarily reflect the views of the publisher, and the publisher hereby disclaims any responsibility for them.

I dedicate this book to all my friends and family

that have looked after me to this day.

Contents

Growing Up In A Village

I was born on 24 May 1973 in Chivhu, a small town in the Midlands area in Zimbabwe. We lived on nearby farms in Mwerari. I was brought up in a family of 11 children; five boys and six girls and we lost about one other child soon after birth, could have been 12. I was the 4th born. Our grandparents and we lived near each other as we had plots which we used to rear our livestock. We had about 14 cattle between us and most of the farming was done using the cattle that we owned, we also owned goats and sheep. Our family was well known in the area. We resided very close to the Buhera-Harare tarred road, and we at times used to buy newspapers from the morning service bus, Matemai, which used to sell us the newspaper, 'The Herald', to keep up with what was happening around the country.

For our lives, we relied on crops which we farmed, and we

used to harvest plenty of very healthy crops. Sometimes it used to be so scary at night trying to move near the fields. Our families used to give each other a hand in planting crops and harvesting with neighbouring families. It was exciting to have all the villagers helping and sometimes, for a brew afterwards, they would slaughter an animal to feed them. The brew was called 'Seven Days' named from the actual days it took for the brew to ferment and become drinkable beer. It's amazing how every household unless religious could make the brew throughout the villages in our area. This was a source of income for most families in the rural villages throughout Zimbabwe. This brew brought families and villagers together as they took time to relax and enjoy themselves catching up with all the village gossip or giving each other ideas on totally different subjects, that could be crop up, jokes and fairy tales were shared during these times. They used to alert villagers of the brew very early in the morning when all the land was quiet and would shout "GOBO." GOBO, which I think was a code to mean we have brew. My parents used to know the voices perfectly well and could tell where the brew was just by hearing the voice of the person shouting. It's amazing how they could identify a person just by their footprints as most used to walk around with no shoes in the dusty roads. It was such a tough life but very exciting at times. We had all sorts of people in our villages, like hunters who used to go hunting all the time and brought lots of game they caught, whose meat was a delicacy to the families of the hunters. Others were into fishing, and I remember doing this with my friends all the time. I used to be a cattle herder and the only time I was freed of this duty was when I was going to school, or at least later in life when my parents managed to get two guys to work for our family in herding cattle and helping with other duties at home.

My father lived in Seke, a city 25 kilometres off Harare. He worked in a water company now known as Quest in Harare, He was a very hard-working man, very aggressive but loving. He managed to bring up all of us from working there. He was the only boy in his family and that I think is the reason why he had many of children to compensate. My mother was religious, but I never saw my father in church. He was rather an alcoholic and smoked a lot. They lived apart all the time but at times my mother would travel to Harare at the end of each month, when my father had been paid from his job and would give my mother some money to take care of us in the village. She would stay for a while and travel back to our rural home with lots of groceries and sometimes clothes and shoes for us to wear. Those were the good times for us. Many people from our villages used to leave their groceries at our home and later would come and collect them with help from their families either in a scotch cart or wheel barrow. There was never a time when those people would find their groceries tampered with, they all found everything intact all the time, we were never jealous of anyone or steal from anyone as we were brought up with strict morals which meant doing anything wrong would make you feel so guilty. And at times, when we did wrong, we were punished severely by both of our parents. I was very naughty, and every time I was punished or beaten up by my parents. It was natural for me to be naughty as the environment we lived in was so tough that you had to be a little bit naughty to live through. That was the reason most parents thought I was naughty. I was not jealous. I grew up with a good heart and many families respected me for this, and I used to have fights with other youngsters who tried to bully me and each time I won. I still have a scar from a fight I had in school with a young boy called Brian, who was so cheeky and he bullied me so much that one day, I thought *'enough is enough'* and I confronted him and a fight ensued. I hit him hard on his forehead causing my hand to get swollen from the impact and he was having a swollen forehead for days. The scars from this is still visible today. From that day onwards, he never tried to bully me again. I never started fights. I was always pushed into them, but when I got angry, I always prevailed in disciplining the bullies.

Droughts were the toughest periods in our lives. We used to travel a long distance to get maize from the government, which was our staple food. They would want to see if you had a partisan card to qualify and because my family was affiliated to the ruling party in Zimbabwe, we were not denied food at all. Our livestock suffered a lot, so we had to take them to a special place where there were plenty of grass for them to feed on, which was called Godzi. That place was in the middle of many farms and to get there, you had to face a lot of obstacles like a farmer called Marefu, who did not allow our livestock to mix with their livestock, some sort of discrimination among village folk and black farmers. What we used to do was drive our cattle slowly towards Godzi using a dusty road paved in-between farms, then as we came towards Marefu's farm we would race our livestock to avoid being stopped and detected, that was fun, but at times we were stopped by a determined Marefu. What could we do? Grass in grazing land in our village would have all dried and not enough to feed our cattle.

Godzi, is a place which was used by farmers as a shopping area and cattle dip and has vast planes with lots of grazing land which was so full of green grass, and after grazing you would see the difference from cattle grazing in the village to those we took to Godzi. The tummies would be visibly full. Sometimes, we would leave the cattle to graze whilst we went down the river fishing and sometimes our cattle would stray into other farms and that's when we got into trouble, but we always came back to Godzi despite the dangers and the hostility between us villagers and the black farmers. I am not saying that we did not get help from black farmers, we did get a lot of stuff from them. They just did not want us to go to Godzi. Because our cattle were said to have diseases which would be passed on to famer's livestock as they were not vaccinated regularly.

The farmers nearby used to engage villagers in helping with farming and would pay them. This was another source of income for villagers. We would get fresh milk or lacto from farms during drought periods and meat and vegetable. We used to buy firewood from these farmers neighbouring us, especially Marimba farm that was close to my home, we were related and they used to help us a lot and we also helped as well, we still get along even today although the farmer is now late.

Christmas in the village was so fun as we got lots of goodies, that was the time we got new clothes or shoes and had rice, chicken and other foods as a feast. We used to go to the growth point and would go from one store to the other in search of fun by watching other people dancing and showing off their dancing skills, getting drunk and making fun of themselves. Afterwards at school, people would be talking about it and sharing the fun they had on Christmas day. It was important not to misbehave as all the people would know about it. It was funny how a silly misbehaviour could find its way through grapevine to all villagers. I think that's how we all used to behave appropriately.

The primary school I went to initially was called Chapisha School. I was so young, when I went to school for the first time to start school and was so naïve, that when I was put in a classroom for grade one, I whistled in class and the teacher shouted, "Who whistled?" He was so angry on me for whistling, and I walked out and went home scared. I never went back again until I was a little bit older. At school, we had to march from our classrooms to the assembly point with drums being played. It was fun and late comers were whipped by teachers. Whipping was the acceptable torture that was used by teachers throughout the schools in Zimbabwe. Some teachers used dusters to hit fingernails. Some used skipping ropes to whip at your legs, and the most used was the small gum tree branches, that was how the teachers disciplined school children. Verbal abuse was common. Most of us behaved well, but did not escape from being whipped at times.

The reason I left school in the rural home to live in the city in Harare was because I had come number one out of all the kids in our class in grade five. My parents were so excited, they offered me a place to study in Seke, a city 25km out of Harare, the capital city of Zimbabwe, as a gesture to show how happy they were by my grades in school, this was in the year 1988.

Escape To Live In The City

Living in the city had always been my dream. I used to dream about it, when I was herding cattle and being harassed by the weather, which was so hot and at times would rain or even get caught in violent weather away from home with thunderstorms. This is the time I always regretted being born. The stress of herding cattle was too much to bear, I used to spend so many times with animals and they do not talk and would just sit idly watching them graze from morning till evening or at times someone came to help out so I could eat my lunch.

In the city, I managed to get a place at Makoni Southern Number 1-Shingisai Primary School. This is where I started my grade six and seven. The school was nice and I loved it. It was not hard to fit in but at times the other kids were involved in lots of mischief outside school like stealing, bullying and some were even Nyawo dancers.

Those days, there was a lot going on in our Makoni and Makoni Southern Community. There was a group of boys or a gang known as 'The Zero Boys'. The gang had a lot of members throughout all the suburbs in Makoni and Makoni Southern, where my school was situated. They were nasty. They used to beat up people in the street for reasons I did not even know, and they used to attract lots of crowd when they did this. They were not afraid of anyone even the police, it seemed as if they were all known to the police but they never got arrested because lots of the victims were very afraid to press charges due to the numbers of the gangs. You could succeed in having a few arrested but you were not even aware of many other members who could come and retaliate and you could get yourself killed. The most notorious thug, one leader of this group was called Farai, he used to wear this mischievous smile on his face when beating up people. He was not scared of height or any person, I saw him beating stalky people than he was. Coming from rural home, where I used to face extreme conditions, I was not afraid of such people and I always wondered why so many people could not fight back. The other scary thing was the numbers of the gang, and at times you could not tell who was from the innocent by-standers or the gang, that's why I came to the conclusion that these guys were not to be messed with.

Most of the kids in my class knew most of the gang, and many were either from families of even so-called car jerkers. Serious members of the Acute-faith Church who were thugs and were involved in clandestine smuggling throughout Africa. The most notorious borders where this smuggling took place was the Zambian border, the border between Zambia and Zimbabwe and the Beit bridge, a border between Zimbabwe and South Africa, there were stories of this sect smuggling goods in coffins pretending to be carrying the dead. Sometimes you would see a brand-new Mercedes Benz parked outside a shark, or a dilapidated house and you would wonder how someone could afford this. Coming from the rural areas with lots of trust and respect to religion, I always thought and regarded religion as 'sacred' but what I was beginning to see through my friends at school was nothing but a shameful religion. I remember a young girl in our class who was married to a member of the sect, someone told me it was normal for young girls to marry at that age to elders of the sect, I was shocked. I was also shocked at the number of women from this sect who owned extended houses but had no husbands, I always wondered what happened to their men. They used to rent out these houses to lots of families, but I do not think they were even taxed for it by the government. I think they just paid rent and few bills and that was it, the rest of the income belonged to them.

Going back to the zero boys, they used to deal in drugs of all sorts, and many would do this in public. Zero boys ruled the streets of Seke. It was the days of breakdancing and some used to wear knuckle-dusters which they used to beat up people with. They ruled the streets. Our teachers were very afraid of them, everyone was. Things always got nasty during schools' sports competitions. That's where they preyed on their enemies from primary to high school, they were nasty.

In my street in Makoni, where I used to stay with my father, we used to live next to a lot of thugs some who later became my friends but not stealing like them but for reasons I don't even understand even now. I was introduced to these guys most of them especially the guy called Dell, who used to reside opposite our house, he was a serious thug, he stole from people shops and all, every now and then he and his thug friends used to congregate put the radio outside his house and they would be talking about all their adventures which I listened to and would be drinking. I think they would have caught a big one and would be celebrating. There was a real story that when he was broke at one time, he went to the shops to steal chicken because he had no money to buy food and he came through an alley way running being chased by people, threw the chicken in his house and ran past and they did not catch him and he came back to have his meal, of course they did not see him throwing the chicken in his house as he left the door open intentionally. For some reason, I was attracted to this sort of life, not that I wanted to steal but I was curious how these guys did their things, I have always been the curious sort.

My own father was a lot strict and would never want me to hang out with these guys and these guys were scared of my father, he was the aggressive sort and was affiliated to ruling party thugs, very dangerous thugs. At one point, I saw a knob carry with blood in our house and I wondered what my father was up to with his gang, they used to go to meetings and all sorts and I did not even attend to those as I was not invited and was not interested, I did not believe in all the madness that was going on, so I kept out from these guys. The only time we went to the gatherings was, when there were Independence celebrations and my father would take us to go and have a feast because he would have contributed, but each time I was disappointed because we would not get anything it was so upsetting, we would get just a little food. I had lots of friends in my neighbourhood and my best friend was John Themba. He was my partner in crime. We tried dating together looking for our future girlfriends. My neighbour house was full of beautiful girls and we used to share a lot together but my father did not want anything to do with them. The most beautiful was Tambu, she was my size, and I adored her. She was nice to me all the time and her sister Tsitsi and her young sister Elizabeth also got on well with me through the ups and downs. We used to play soccer with my friend John. Football money games were so popular around those days and John used to make sure I was included in those games and we used to win but when it came to more professional matches, John was better than me, but I used to accompany him to football matches. He was good at tackles, the boy was aggressive at the back, he was a defender. John and I were very close there is nothing that we didn't do together.

One day, my brother Tom was playing outside our house in the street, when he was beaten by this street boy called Evans. Everyone was so afraid of him. He had this fancy street persona and that made me feel backward at times from my rural upbringing. He talked in slang and that made me feel inferior, but when I heard that he beat my brother, I was so angry that I did not care about anything but to confront him. I went towards where my brother was playing and saw Evans and I quickly confronted him, but a guy called Tafara, a friend of Evans, tried to intervene and we started exchanging blows and each time I hit him he fell to the ground, that was when Evans tried to join in that made my friend John to support me, the fight stopped with Tafara on the floor and everyone laughing. From that day, no one messed with me and that was the downfall of Evans, he never behaved that way ever again.

John was a bit naughty and I remember one day in the evening he was beating his niece and he was confronted by a thug who lived down our street. "Don't beat up ladies," he shouted and hit John. John fell down and as he was trying to stand up, he was kicked in the face and he fell flat unresponsive. *'John is dead',* I thought. The thug just went away and disappeared in the night. Everyone including me went back to the house, I did not know what to do. I saw Tsitsi crying and trying to resuscitate John. I checked later and was told that John was okay, that was scary. The year 1993 was a crazy year. Everybody was trying to imitate their favourite celebrity on TV through dressing. Most of the youngsters were into pop and hip-hop music and dressed like gangsters. In Seke, boys were being naughty and there was street violence everywhere. Dancing was a favourite pass time for many and discos were prominent. There were a lot of gangs that clashed at every Saturday disco at Manhenga Hotel and throughout the neighbourhoods like Seke and Makoni Southern. The old and middle aged were into local music bands which they came to see at Manhenga Hotel and local beerhalls in all the neighbourhoods. People used to drink so much and there were lots of promiscuity among the old folks and a lot of marital problems caused by misuse of money they were supposed to use to look after their families. Skint youngsters were also caught up in the craze and used to drill holes through the durawalls just to get a glimpse of their favourite musician in action and the craze inside the hall where the music was playing. It was so crazy. No wonder, I changed from a nice innocent guy to naughty in a short period of time. In Seke, people used to confuse me, on the other hand they would engage in immoral tendencies but if a woman was caught cheating with another man's wife, she was severely punished by a mob of angry people throwing stones and all sorts. Thieves' received mob justice the same way if caught stealing. I witnessed a lot of thieves being severely beaten by mobs; being trampled on and kicked, it was a nasty sight. Thieves' also killed lots of people in the night coming from clubs and robbed them going to town, people used to engage in running battles with each other, pushing and shoving and trying to get into busses which were quite a few than the numbers wanting to get to town, it was known as 'pressure'. It was a nasty sight and dangerous, but became normal throughout my life in Seke.

My favourite pass time was going to watch movies at Manhenga Hotel. The situation during the days was mad, young man and some older than me used to queue up to see the movies, disco or bands like Lee Matsito, named Mr Seke, that were popular at that time. The conference room where the videos were played was so large it accommodated approximately 200 people. Sometimes when there was a good movie, I would not manage to get in because the place will be full and they turned people away, it was such an exciting period. The guy called Toto, a very funny and short man who played the videos would say all sorts of obscene words if people were noisy or disruptive, he used to call us 'Sons of Beaches' and he used to get away with that, of course we didn't care all we wanted was to see the movies. I had two friends who were brothers, Peter and Josh, they were the doormen for this movie conference and each time when full and everyone was being turned away, they would smuggle me in. I do not know up to today why these guys liked me so much but they were nice to me. Sometimes, when I was breaking with no money, they would smuggle me in to watch the movies for free. No women came to watch the movies, only a few, each time women came they were subjected to a lot of hostility, everyone would go "whema whema", meaning pussy. I used to watch the evening and night movies as well. This happened when my father had gone to his night shift. As soon as he left the house, I was also on my way to go to the movies, because they started at 8 pm, I used to walk in the dark streets at midnight when everyone was all asleep. After the movies, it was scary, but the adrenaline would make me want more. John was not a movie person but was jealousy to know I was going to the movies. Many times, they tried to stop me. As there were thugs around living in the neighbourhood, each time I came from the movies my heart would be racing thinking, what if someone has broken into our home what would I say to my father. One night, when I was coming from the movie in the night, I saw sofa cushions on our fence and lots of torn pieces of clothing hanging on the gate. My heart sank. I thought, *'That's it, our house has been robbed'.* I opened the gate and went inside quickly checked everything and found everything intact. It was a prank by John. I went outside and removed all the things that were put on our fence and went to sleep. One day, I left my young brother at home to go to watch a night movie. He did not manage to sleep, waiting for me, and he was using a candle. We used to use candles for light at night and paraffin stoves to cook and did not have fridge. The candle was burning and was on the table and was running out, when nearly about to burn the table, my father arrived before me and took my sleeping brother to bed. I was in trouble. The following morning, he asked me where I had been and I told him, he was so angry that he took his police constabulary button stick and hit me several times with it that left so many blisters on my body. I stopped going to movies at night but continued with daytime movies. The money I used was pocket money for food in the house, as my mother lived in the country in our rural home, so I was in charge of the entire kitchen and cooking for the family that's why I had money all the time. I watched all sorts of movies from horror to many Vietnam War movies, World War movies, Sylvester Stallone's, Arnold Schwarzenegger, Steven Seagal, ninja, karate and kungfu of all sorts.

I used to go watching movies as well in the Makoni Southern Hall with my friend Nico from my high school days, the hall smelled of wee and I saw many kungfu movies there on a very large screen and at one point, the hall was used to train karate with my friend Fox. My Sincere was John Mapfunde who had a black belt in karate.

Nico and I were best friends at high school, he was shy and was a talented artist who could reproduce any picture before him, he was also a break-dancer and was good in martial arts. He also hanged around nasty people and my father liked him for reasons I am not aware but looks like he knew my father's side chick. High school was the best time for me, we enjoyed hip-hop especially from the 90s, and music on radio was good and everyone was into music. We even had song books that we used to write music lyrics and I can still rap the song 'Ice, Ice Baby' from Vanilla Ice song to Shabba ranks songs and Madonna like a prayer and many other including Michael Jackson songs.

My first date was Lynette Chaponda, who left me with a

broken heart after she agreed to date me and then I found out she was dating another guy, I nearly had a heart attack. I had trouble in trying to woo the girl and having succeeded she then let me down, she was so beautiful and I loved everything about her and I used to sing the song 'Princess' from the spin doctors just to remind myself of her. Then I met Juliet who is now my wife and we did not date straight away when we were at high school. She was then transferred to Marondera Boarding School. I found out from her friend and tracked her and we communicated through mail. One of the holidays, I was admitted in hospital, when I was working for Quest. After finishing high school, found out she fancied me. I was admitted and my appendix was removed. I suspect food poisoning. When I came from hospital, she sent me a get-well-soon card and the rest is history. The dating had begun. I tried to date so many women; from my sister's beautiful maid Martha to Mercy Jomti and many other girls, but Juliet stood the test. Each time felt out of love from the girls I tried to date, because they were timing other people. I really loved Juliet who is now my wife with all my heart and still do. The thing I love about her is difficult to say, but I just feel it when she is around and when she is not, I feel empty. She had this family behind her. I never knew, she was connected and she was faithful or not she must hide it quite well. Some other girls tried to force themselves on me like my sister's maid. Onetime, she came to me when I was sleeping near the sink area on the kitchen floor at our house in Seke, came and put her feet astride over my face and when I took my face out of blankets trying to find out what was happening, my face was inside her skirt, I jumped out surprised, that was scary. I also fell in love head over heels with my sister Rita's maid who was so beautiful, but the relationship was so short-lived as my brother Clive became interested in her. Martha told me that she was being introduced to his friends as his girlfriend. I was so naïve that I got so angry and dumped her, soon afterwards my father passed away and when coming back from the funeral in our rural home, I started thinking about reconciling with her. When I arrived excitedly at our house in Seke, where we had left her to look after our home, she had another man with her. I was so angry, and I took off angrily to Mabvuku, where I was now living in Harare.

Afterwards I fell in love with a young girl called Mercy Jomti. We met after I had been double-crossed by another girl. I was trying to date and our love continued for a while until I lost my job at Quest, I just fell out of love with the girl for many reasons that I cannot understand till now. She was impregnated after I took a back seat in the relationship. I met her one day, and I was surprised to see that she was heavily pregnant. That was the last time I met her and I remember she tried to reach to me through Facebook recently, I am not sure why but crazy things have been happening, so I am not surprised why my exes have been behaving crazy towards me wanting to force their way into my life.

During high school, I had a friend who was stabbed with a screwdriver and he died. The violence was too much in our schools and at one time, I was walking with my friends from school, those were the days of wrestling and I was holding a Hucksall Jim Dugan wood plank. When a gang of about six boys came to us and one of them demanded the plank I was holding, he said, "Give me that now." I said no and he tried to grab it, and I was so angry I gave him a hard slap on his cheek and sprinted away. He tried to chase me and everyone started laughing at him, he stopped. That day, I was so lucky, if they were determined they could have me done but they did not expect me to do that. Makoni 1 High School was the name of the school I went to do my high school. I was also selected at one time to go and do mass displays at the Independence Day in the Gwanzura Stadium. We were trained by one of the aids of President Simon Matadza called 'Soko' which means monkey. He used to come to us riding a motor bike, he was acrobatic. He was a cheeky man together with his team of combatants, he used to threaten to get all our pants torn from rigorous marching, we went through a very rigorous training and we performed at Independence Day celebrations, our act was called 'The Shield Chapter', he was happy with our act. It went smoothly. After this, we were given tommies to wear and meat pies to eat but they forgot about us.

We used to have a headmaster known as Mativha, he was famous for slapping. If he found anyone loitering at school or making noise during school time or late for school, he would slap you, oh my god, this man terrorised school children with his slapping, everyone including myself was slapped once.

There was this lady teacher who sent me and another boy for being mischievous in class to her friend male teacher for beating. The male teacher took us to his class, laughed about the idea and sent us back without beating us and said to her, "I have brushed them." That was funny I guess till today she thinks the teacher brushed us. When we were about to write our O-Levels, I picked up a letter from the class and I thought it was a romantic letter, so I took it out it in my bag and went home. Whilst at home, I remembered the letter, opened it and found out that it was packed with money about Z$700 for school fees. My heart sank and without thinking twice I took the money back to school and gave it to my form teacher Mr Jackson and he was surprised. The money belonged to a girl called Dexter. Imagine if she had lost that money for good, she could have had not written her ordinary levels. Her life could have been doomed. She was not from a rich family. I was rewarded by being made a librarian for being trust worth. Some people thought I was foolish but that did not faze me as I did the same to two more people later in life as I will explain later.

Mbiri Musika is a place where all people coming from the rural areas use as their arrival and departure station. The place is a nasty place to be in Africa. Thieves wreak havoc and steal in broad day light. I dreaded every minute of going to that place. Many people in Zimbabwe lost a lot of things. Foreigners stay completely out from this area. I happened to be walking from the city of Harare library in the heart of Harare when me and my friend Rodney Chitisi in our school uniforms were walking in Mbiri Musika, when suddenly we were approached by a guy who grabbed Rodney's hand around the wrist and then let it go, then he passed us only to realise he had snatched Rodney's digital watch from his wrist. The move was so fast to know what had happened. Rodney ran after him and grabbed him, tears running down his face and crying. "Give back my watch, give back my watch," he cried holding on to this stalky guy. I was so confused, I just stood by Rodney. The thief lifted his shirt to scare us and we could see a very long knife tucked inside his trousers. Rodney continued to cry and would not let go. That was scary. The thief then released his watch and gave it back to Rodney. We walked away and nobody came to our rescue, the watch nowadays cannot even cost a pound, it's ridiculous what thieves those days could steal, if it was good money we were as good as dead.

My First Job

Since leaving high school, I was sent back to our rural home to herd cattle. For a while at our rural home I was herding cattle when my big sister Martha Matatu contacted me before we received our ordinary level results to say she had found me a job at Quest in Harare's Five Street branch. I prepared my stuff and said goodbye to my mother and headed for Harare. I left Innocent and Phibion my father's handymen with the job.

I met my sister in Harare, and she took me to her Five Street office, where we went to fill in the forms and there, I met Tucson, who had just come out of jail for fraud together with Zimbabwe's prominent musician Roger Chikundu. Tucson and Roger Chikundu were friends and he even asked Chikundu to our Quest offices when we started work. Tucson defrauded me out of my school fees to supplement my studies after I was employed in

Quest. He took the money after we began studies to improve our grades since there were many chances of promotion in Quest. I trusted Tucson to enrol me at a local school for my O-Level and I only realised he had cheated me after I was due to write the exams. I realised that I had been conned and it was heart breaking. I had wasted all my time studying for nothing. I was employed as a labourer and I worked in the Quest head offices at Five Street in Harare; I managed to meet a team of crazy human beings I have ever met, from pimps, hookers and gays, we used to work as one family in the dispatch, sharing food under the watchful eyes of a crazy old man called Mr Mugezi, who is now late. I remember at one time being taught about marriage by Mr Mugezi and used to share his sleazy sex stories with us. He used to date a disabled woman other than his normal wife, who only came to work. One day, I found him having sex with her in our office during one of our overtime weekends at the head office. I was shocked. I fell from a table I was climbing on; she was using a directory as pillow. That was a sight for sore eyes. Mr Mugezi was an old man with grey hair throughout who was obsessed with sex stories. I remember in that office, relationships were made and broken with each party trying to prove they were man enough and ended up marrying older women or relationships which were not workable. My big boss called Muroyiwa was a womaniser. On Valentine's Day, office was filled with flowers from different women. That was crazy; bees could be seen buzzing in his office because of the flowers.

In Quest, lots of guys did not do their work properly. Meter readers were estimating readings instead of going to actually reading meters physically; some were reversing meters colluding with customers for quick buck and go to a place near Chegutu called Bora to spend their proceeds away from prying eyes. Chegutu is a town outside of Harare. In offices, people were destroyed by loan sharks, the late Chivaraidze was one of the notorious men who used to lend lots of money to staff in Quest and because they had access to their wages' payslips, they could tell how much they had earned and took all of it off them. Men used to borrow more than they were earning and each time they were giving all their wages to the loan sharks and then borrowing money to feed their families.

Chivaraidze used violence in order to recover his money. At one point, I was also caught up in this vicious circle when I was looking after my brother Clive who had lost his job. I was in desperate need of money to support him, so I ended up borrowing until all my money was sucked by loan sharks. We lived in Mabvuku in Harare, near Airport road to a house belonging to Mr Preza.

I had to borrow again to have money for food and the circle continued, until one day, when I had to resign following allegations that I had committed a fraud of having used a cheque to pay for a water bill for my friend who had given me cash, but unfortunately the cheque was returned unpaid. Despite me having rights for it to be paid because my bank account, had an overdraft facility. The facility was withdrawn causing this problem and I tried to cover it up leading to it being picked up by credit control. I quickly resigned from my job because nobody could understand what was happening to me at that time. I blame the loan sharks. The loan sharks that used to lend me money were Lino, who worked for Quest in the payroll building, and I think he did accounts for Harare division. Kaseke was another one who worked in the payroll building as a senior salaries officer. He knew our salaries before I even had a chance to look at the payslip, so he used this position to take all the money from us. There were other loan sharks like a guy called Paul, who loaned us as well but did not work for Quest. Month end was the worst period to be at work, as these guys came hunting for us wanting their money. We would play hide and seek with these guys. Each time we noticed them coming we would disappear fast and our bosses knew what was happening and did not bother at all about looking for us. Sometimes lots of absences at month end was the norm as we tried to escape from the harassment of these guys; they circled like vultures. Sometimes you would give all your wages to one and borrow again as soon and pay another and borrow again. Sometimes these guys would refuse to borrow same day and that was when all hell broke loose as you could not pay the others and that meant playing hide and seek until you were paid.

Quest had lots of characters from people who were alcoholics to those indebted to loan sharks. Alcoholics like a guy called Kuda, would not report for days after getting wages. He would not phone in or report why he was not coming to work. He would come to work when all the money was gone from drinking, I think he was also afraid of getting all the money from his wages taken by loan sharks. Our manager would have arranged a loan for him from loan sharks that meant he was afraid to contact the manager in case he would ask for the loan shark's money. When he finally came to work, the manager never fired or punished him.

Usually the loan sharks would give up looking for you after a week from the day you get your wages as they knew you would not have money to pay them after this period; they would wait until another month end to come hunting for you. A loan shark known as Chivaraidze or Dave used violence to get his money; I saw some very aged people treated like kids being poked and harassed by him. He was a nasty piece of work and he had this look on his face which was stone cold. He was scary, but for some reason he did not treat me the same way; he was lenient and I kept going to borrow. He is now deceased but I still owed him after I left Quest.

Working for Quest was exciting. We were known as the highly paid people in the town and people used to look up to us. Nobody knew about the problems we had with loan sharks, they just saw the uniforms and treated us as though we were sitting pretty and having it all. Only the people we worked with knew about what was happening and sometimes you would forget there was trouble month end. We used to have lunch as a team which was cooked by a guy called Munyebvu, or 'Soldier', and we called the lunch race. We used to share the same plates as a group of about ten people. Race brought us together, managers and employees, we were very close. Each member contributed a dollar or two to buy meat and mealie meal to cook our lunch. Munyebvu was a good cook. Sometimes he would let me eat even when I had not paid.

I can actually say working for Quest was the best thing that ever happened to me. I learnt to use computers when most of my peers were not able to operate a terminal. As I joined Quest in the dispatch, we used to send water bills to customers and this job involved packing bills into the envelopes and franking them, delivered them to our local postal office and that's it. I was promoted to a data capturing job in the data capture office, where we used to input or capture meter readings from meter reading books into the computer ready for billing. It required accuracy and speed. I became very fast at inputting meter readings into the terminals. There was lots of fun in this office; we were all young and I tried dating two girls same time in the same office. I only succeeded to take one out for a date. The girl's name was Rita Munyoro, a daughter of one of our senior managers. She had a boyfriend in South Africa and was always going to see the gynaecologist which scared me a lot as I thought she was somehow ill. This made our date not to go any further, I was scared of contracting Aids, so we did not click. The other girl, Peggy liked me so much. She was fit, but she had a nasty scent that seemed to come from her private parts that discouraged me from making a move, but the girl liked me. She ended up dating my friend called Sidney and he came back and said he tried to have sex with the girl and she had cotton wool stuffed in her vagina which was smelling awful and made him to stop; he never dated her again. The problem I think was lack of proper sanitary pads for women to use during a period or I am sure, lots of girls had the same issue. In my lifetime, I tried to date lots of girls, but lots of them were not my type, most of it was just for fun. I dated girls in each suburb in our town and at Quest; we used to work on the frontline. After I was promoted to a customer service representative job, we used to look out for beautiful girls coming to enquire about their water bills and we used that opportunity to pounce on these beautiful girls. The thing about it was that once they come to you, you would know where they lived with their telephone numbers, so it was easy to date them. Only a few dates succeeded but the rest were just not right, but it was fun. Lots of people envied me as I used to dress really nice and smart. They used to call me all sorts of nick names like 'senior', 'teacher' or 'professor'. We used to compete on dressing and there was this guy called Rodgers, who used to dress really nice like a manager. He used to call himself

'Management'; he was a funny guy. His problem was he was scared of women. He was that sort who could not join in the fun like we did. He just did try when everyone was watching but could not bring himself to chatting seriously for a relationship, and we used to call these guys 'Appetizers'. There was another guy called Allen Makuti, who used to dress like Michael Jackson. He was just a quiet man, but we used to joke with him about not being interested in women; we called him appetizer as well. Then there was a guy called Bright Dupwa; the guy ended up marrying an older woman who was also my former boss. When I was in data capture, after a contest, where everyone was trying to prove being macho. Bright tried to prove that he was man enough and they ended up sleeping together and ended up marrying each other. Everyone was surprised and got very worried. It was one of the jokes that went wrong. The reason I say this is that one day, I was discussing this relationship by someone and he got to hear about it and he got so upset he took me outside the Quest office and gave me a hard slap on my cheek for gossiping about him. I will never forget that day. I felt stupid and embarrassed. There was also another guy called Tofara Mutiti, this guy was very funny, he imitated the bosses. He made fun of everyone and he was so naughty. He was the type who would kick your tea bread as a ball or show his manhood to everyone in the office, including women, of course he did that. He wrecked motor bikes and was demoted a few times from his job, and the last time he worked for Quest was when he was promoted to work as a cashier at one of the satellite offices, and it was him and the security guard in that office to protect the funds collected. He is said to have asked the security guard to go and buy him some buns for tea at the shops, the guard went to do so and brought some buns and Tofara told him they were very stale he should go back and buy fresh ones. When the guard came back, Tofara told him that thieves came and stole thousands of dollars. Crazy this guy is a proper nut case. Every time I speak with him, he is always trying to bring up my case with Quest when I resigned, he calls me a thug.

To show that I am not really a thief, one day I was working on the front line at the Five Street branch of Quest, when a guy came to enquire about his bill which he thought was inflated, I handled the enquiry so well that he was impressed and was so happy he left an envelope containing about a thousand dollars, I only noticed the envelope when he was gone. I was surprised and I gave it to my sister who was the manager at that office, Mrs Matatu. The guy came back later looking for his money. I received a letter of praise for honesty to customers from the senior commercial engineer in Quest, Mr Muzembi. It seemed people started conspiring after this as everyone was dirty and did not want people like me around.

At one time, I started living in Toby street in Mabvuku, after my brother was arrested on charges of fraud. Remember I told you of a time, we rented Mr Preza's house near airport road. My brother tried to defend himself, after he was charged with fraud at work, but he failed. I looked after him for a while and I think this is the same reason why I got into debt further as it was the first time I was looking after someone, taking care of all the bills and food. It was my first job and had never done this before, so I was so naïve as I thought my brother was going to get his job back, he never did so I ended up going to live on my own. In Toby Street, I shared the same house with a family that was good but strange. They used to do all the cleaning in my room and cook for me. In the next room resided a nasty guy called Mike; this guy brought different women every day in his room on a daily basis. I developed a liking to him and discovered after a while that he was using different cars every day and I wondered if he was a government agent or not. After a while, I tried to see what this guy did and I asked for a lift in one of his cars, a VW Golf to work. He called himself Nightrider, from the TV Program 'Nightrider'. He agreed and set for the city. The guy was a very tremendous driver and reckless. In the morning, there was a queue of cars leading to the city and he drove so fast, and each time avoided the queues by overtaking cars going through gaps left by motorists when driving between the other. Each time he did this he would bring a mischievous smile on his face, I enjoyed it; I loved adventure. He played Usher's new album Nice and slow that time. He took me to his offices at Hurudza house, where I saw a bunch of girls who were waiting for him. The guy was a ladies' man. I only realised that the guy was actually a car jerker. The last time I saw him, he was pursued by CID police officers from the house but they failed to catch up with him in a car chase that was extreme, and his car was wrecked to bits and he ended up on foot and disappeared in the suburbs in Mabvuku. I only left this house soon afterwards after I was accused of using another Quest employee's water benefit and not giving him anything. The water benefit allowed me to live in low-density suburbs, as we were allowed a certain amount of hundred dollars' worth of benefit which we could connect at our landlord home and used. The landlord would ask us to pay little or no rent, as we took care of their water bill. You could also use a friend's benefit if they were not using it and that is what I was caught doing after I failed to pay the beneficiary amount we had agreed, so that I could use his benefit. I was reported to police and the case was dropped after rigorous questioning by a detective at Southern Police Station. CID Officer Ruben who was going out with my sister at that time managed to have the case thrown out, I was very lucky.

Hustle In The City Of Harare

When I left Quest, I was so relieved of the pressure which was on me. I remember my father passed away just afterwards. He had been so ill for a very long time. I don't know what was going on, but it was devastating. It was like my whole world was crumbling down. That time, I had been living alone in Belvedere near the civic centre in Vito Close. I used to rent a small room just outside the main home of a lady who worked for the TM stores in Harare. She had three beautiful girls living with her. Those days, I was hanging around with Moses, who was on contract from Quest. Moses was also a womaniser. We used to drive around in his friend's car, whose name was Langton and he worked for Cimas as a general manager; Langton, a serial womaniser as well. And the time I went around with these guys, they tried to have me take some of their ladies. I remember going with Langton and Moses to Marimba and we picked up two girls along the way. When we went to a disco at Circus Club in Harare, we danced for a while and one of the girls was Moses's girlfriend and the other was her friend—I think the daughter of a government official, she was from a rich family. She asked us to take her to Marimba in Borrowdale, so we set for Borrowdale. She was after her boyfriend who had just left her to go there. We arrived at Marimba, and at first, we were not allowed in as it was a members-only club. It was full of white people and a few blacks and the atmosphere was totally mad, people were dancing and each time they finished drinking a glass of beer, they would smash it, on the floor, loud rave music was playing and I had never seen anything like that, the floor was littered with broken glass from smashed glass. We found the guy she wanted and he looked like Morpheus in the Metrix movie.

We left her there and went back home. I remember this other time there was a show at the Harare show grounds. After the show me and Moses managed to chat with two girls who were going in the same direction to town. After we got to town, me and the other girl started kissing. I remember it was so romantic that she started singing the song 'All my Love' from Jodeci! Moses became jealous, and he called Langton on his phone and when Langton arrived, he started kissing my girl. I was so furious and the girl apologised, but I was fuming. That was the last time I had any contact with Langton. The reason was that Langton had a car and I did not. It was a brand-new Mazda 626 Cronos. I still had contact with Moses though. We used to go to a place called Snow Hill in the heart of Harare and spent money on video games. Snow Hill was a big complex with many food outlets at the bottom and on top floor, there was a space for dining and another was filled with video games and pool tables. This became one of our meeting and playgrounds. Whenever we were bored, I would go to town from Seke and meet Moses there. Moses was also obsessed with playing video games. I remember there was a kungfu video game that he was obsessed with. He would play the game so much that he would start sweating like he was doing some manual labour or something strenuous. That's how obsessed he was. Many of the staff knew us. We also played pool which was so popular among the young man those days. It was so popular that to challenge someone to play, the game usually took hours of waiting as many other people would be queuing to play. Moses was so good at playing pool and I was average. I learnt how to handle the stick quite well. Moses had so many techniques that he used to sink the balls, he was unbeatable and that's what I enjoyed about him. If you got into a habit of winning all the time, you could get some respect from other guys you played with. Moses worked for National Tyres those days. It was a company that sold tyres for cars. He was in charge of selling new tyres to its customers and this is where he got most of his spare cash, by selling car tyres in the black-market to get pocket money. It was a type of fraud that was common in every business and store around Harare, involving employees. Most of the people who did this were underpaid so they used to get extra money by selling company stock to their friends or customers illegally for half the price of the item. On a good day, Moses would have around $500, and that was a lot of money back then. We would go to and from uptown clubs and play pool and go home late at night. The other clubs which we went to was Club Liz which was a nice club with beautiful girls throughout and waitresses wearing miniskirts. It was just nice patronising in the club but we hardly got anything to do with the girls. It was just a good place to be for a young man as I was those days.

When I left Quest, the whole world became so difficult for me. When I thought I was free, I was wrong. The freedom turned out to be a nightmare. I started looking for work until all my shoes were ripped from walking up and down. The job I found was to do with selling stationery. I had been working for Quest as a customer sales representative, so I thought I could do any job along those lines. I was so naïve those days. Jobs were hard to come by, so I was recruited as a salesman by a guy called Tendai Munyoro for his small business called Vital Stationery. Tendai Munyoro was a con artist. When he employed me and other guys, we thought we were lucky to be employed by him. What we did not know was that this guy was a broker. He did not own the products he sold. All he did was, he would get orders and take them to a local wholesaler of stationery and buy them at a low price and resale them at a higher price. He would not tell us that was the case. We only realised by mistake after working for a while in his business. He gave us price lists to go and sale the stationery to buyers of big companies across the city. Each time, we hardly got any orders. At the end of the month, Tendai would take one by one to a corner in his office away from other people and pretend like he was going to pay you a salary but never did. All he did was ask you how many orders you got or sold like he did not know, and if you said none he would smile and told you that there was nothing that he could pay you because there was no fixed salary on the job. It was so upsetting but we stayed working for him still. Then I noticed other guys were just like me using his office to while up time and looking for other prospects or mischief. We used to use the business to gain access to all high-profile businesses, not only to sell his products but to befriend people in high-profile jobs like buyers of businesses and try to get employed in those businesses. Sometimes, we would just go and chat to girls who were secretaries of other businesses just to while up time, with the aim of trying to get prospects to get employed one day. To get employed you would know somebody who knew somebody in a high position to do that. That is why, we ended up using Vital to get to that. Sometimes, we would stop working and Tendai bought us beer and we would drink and while up time. We became good friends. This is where I learnt tricks of the trade in business and I have since set up my business with the name Vital to remind me of the days I learnt to hustle in business. The business is now called Vital Oven Cleaners Ltd. The whole city was full of companies like this and girls were being exploited the same way. They would pretend to be going to work but when in actual fact they were working for sex to get money to feed their families. I would see people who would crowd at the telephone exchange, known as CTC, taking turns to call relatives and friends abroad looking for easy money and dealing. I ended up recognising the faces which were always doing these things every day. I once met a schoolmate from high school who had his thriving business. He was into repairing mobile phones. Each time someone brought a broken mobile phone he would repair it. It was a lucrative business for someone who knew how to repair them. Sometimes Rodney would repair and sell the mobile phones from his customers, as mobile phones were in demand, especially Sony Ericson's. He would pretend to have lost the phone. He dismantled the phones soon after he got it for repair so that it was not easy to identify it, and he ended up giving the customer another phone from another customer to cover up. He received lots of stolen phones from criminals which he dismantled and sold to other people. One day, I was so broke and I asked for one of the phones to sell for a profit. The phone was bought but I ended up using all the money. Rodney finally caught me when I was now employed and threatened to have me arrested. I had money that day and I gave him all the money that I had; it was scary. I was trying to get into a movie when he caught me. Trouble used to catch up with me those days, no matter I was being nice or not.

Probert Children's Club

When I left Vital Stationery, I was on the verge of a breakdown psychologically. I was tired of Hustle and getting nowhere. This is when I came across another club that helped young children from the streets and helping them stay off streets and reuniting some with their families. I took on the chance and this to me was a chance given by God to redeem myself from all the bad things I had done. I thought I had been punished and it was a way of paying back. I wanted to help poor little kids to get back on their feet after being let down by the system.

I spoke to the owner of the club who was called Mrs Law. The patron of the club was the former footballer Tennyson Maramba. She agreed that I come to her club and help with caring for the street kids; I prefer to call them street children. I started helping out for free, looking after the street children at the club. The club is situated in the centre of Harare opposite Mohadi Hotel in 4th avenue. The club used a big hall at the Probert Church in Harare City Centre. The set up was like a club. There was Mrs Law, as the head of the club and there was a social worker Mrs Trudy, who worked with the children. I came to know that Mrs Law went to the same school as President Simon Matadza, and they were known to each other and was a member of his party's women league. Expatriates and foreign visitors came to this club to fund it and also help out as volunteers. We had a few local volunteer teachers who were also employed by Mrs Law. I started to work there and enjoyed every little time I was working there. I came to love all the street children there. I was so close to two boys; one from Seke where I came from called Sipho and one from Epworth called Trey. These children were very intelligent, more than the average kids I have met in my life. They were so talented; I also became friends with a volunteer called Kidwell and another called Prince. Kidwell was not interested in the kids at all and he only was interested in the stipend that he was getting which was called honorarium. Prince taught the kids to do batik and other crafts. There was also a single women's club running alongside this one and as well as a home for street children situated a few miles from Harare called Broadway House. This was looked after by a guy called Bernard and another called Donald. Both guys had no passion in what they were doing and only came to get gifts from Foreigners who were coming to his club and dates with white women. There was so much jealous that was seen between these guys. Being poor were the drive to make these guys to be interested only in money from foreigners and they competed to get the one who was rich. They nearly had me killed by the street children but the children refused to carry out the dirty work and told me the plan. Some of them did not want to be seen walking with street children but I did. I was enthusiastic and many of them felt I was real. You know what, children can tell easily if you love them or not. After a while working with these children, I met Mrs White who had come to visit Zimbabwe from America. She and her husband were nice people and I used to work with Mrs White, and she saw how passionate I was that she invited me, Sipho and Trey to a town hotel where they had been staying called Gekhos. I went there and she showered us with presents together with her husband. They treated us like human beings and I was very happy to be treated as such. Although I sold the presents to raise money for bus fare as no one was paying for my bus fare from Seke to Harare every day. I had to sacrifice to go and teach these kids. Mrs White and husband asked me why I was involved with teaching and I told her that I was sacrificing everything to work at the club and she offered to pay me US$100 a month in wages from her own pocket which she did for quite a long time until I left the club paid directly to Mrs Law. After a while, Mrs Law was told of the arrangement and she was so happy and she started to pay me a stipend, known as honorarium at the end of each month. This was not enough but it was better than nothing. Mrs Law discovered I was good with accounts so she introduced me to do her bookkeeping which I did until I left the club being accused of having stolen some money. There was a lady called Emma who was also Swedish who looked after the kids fulltime. I became very good friends with her as she saw how passionate I was with these children. She introduced me to a local group of singers well known in Zimbabwe called Mhofu. The leader of the group is called teacher, they had programmes with the children teaching them arts and dance and I was once involved with them as they were teaching dance to one of the club's older boys named Knowledge, the boy was crazy, he thought he was in love with

Emma, that is the problem I had working at the club: everybody seemed to be interested in exploiting one or the other. I worked very well with Emma taking children off the street and reuniting them with their parents. Being assigned to a bookkeeper was one problem that took me off from concentrating on working directly with the children. My money problems became high as I was paid less than I could afford to live by so I started using some of the money that I was in charge of and returning it after I was paid this continued until I was sacked by Mrs Law, but I do not think that was the reason. The reason was I found out Mrs Law books were not being properly run and she was using lots of the money from donations for her own use, when I left the club, she gave me a good reference. Why would someone do that if I was a thief. Whilst at Probert Club, I met an American girl called Johanne. She was so beautiful, and I fell for her. We became close friends, but there was also another local celebrity who was after her called Lloyd. He was always turning up at the club and was spoiling everything. Sometimes I would meet the two together and that broke my heart. I was in love with Juliet now my wife at that time so that caused me to stop being serious with her as well. One day, we went clubbing and she gave me her keys. I realised she was into me but somehow, I blew it later when I gave her back the keys and allowed her to go back home by herself. I stayed at the Tube club until late and slept on the streets because I could not find a bus late at night to take me home. I had no money, that's the reason why I felt bad, she funded everything; and the other thing she had told me that she was a lesbian, I was confused. She was a party girl. She finally went back to the America and we communicated a little until Lloyd visited America and told me he was in love with her. She is now married to someone else and has kids. I met another lady called Leona and I remember we became good friends. One day we went to visit Nyanyadzi together. I had a cousin brother who worked in Nyanyadzi. We went to stay with him and we used to share a bed and room with Leona. It was a very complicated relationship but we were not in love. She was not happy to have us have a relationship. In Nyanyadzi, we saw the local people being terrorised by elephants at night, we also saw a few elephants on a walking safari in Nyanyadzi and we went swimming at Masori Hotel. Back in Harare, Leona introduced me to Brian, a local singer in Harare. We played cards called crazy 8 and I beat them all several times. We remained friends until she returned to Holland. Mrs Trudy tried to set me up with a girl from the streets that she was looking after. The young girl was having her school fees paid by someone from the UK or so I think, and she was at Harare High School in Harare, an upper-class school. I was asked to have with her extracurricular lessons and found out she was not interested in that and she wanted to have a general chitchat with me. I was put off and I tried to stir everything to school work and I remember telling Mrs Trudy that she was not interested in getting taught and she never came to me again. I remember her singing the TLC song to me, 'No Scrubs', which gave me the idea she was just after an affair nothing else. I did not believe in exploiting street children so I ended up not teaching her again.

Big Carpets

remember working for this business that sold carpets and did carpet cleaning after I had left Probert's Club. I was a sales man for them selling their carpets and carpet cleaning services. The thing was I was so broke, that I wanted my commission for each job I did like now, and I ended up receiving my commission late. I was tempted to collect money from a job we had done and I disappeared because the owner of Big Carpets was not paying me on time, he was exploitative. One day, they caught up with me and they manhandled me and put me into their van, took me to their shop. I thought I was going to get beaten but they did not, they simply took off my shoes and asked me to go and find the money I had taken and come to get my shoes. I walked bare foot through the city of Harare and to the industries where my brother worked. My brother Timothy, who was the third born in our family had a good job, working for Harare Home Stores. I told him what had happened and he gave me money and I paid them back and got my shoes back. It was crazy. At one time, I lived with my brother Timothy, in Kuwadzana in Harare. Whilst staying with him, there was this girl who lived next door who had a baby who I came to know as Lucy. She was a young girl who had just had a child in her teens. I developed a like for her and she invited me once into her home, we had sex and it was just a one-night stand and I never went back again.

After a while, I started working with a guy called Freddy, as a salesperson, for his carpet cleaning business. He was professional and we used to meet in a wimpy shop for a cuppa and discuss all the business, it was fun. The thing about Freddy was that he had no proper equipment. He had a big vacuum machine and a couple of dishes and brushes. Each time I got a job we would go and fill the buckets, put a detergent, produce a foam and splash it on the carpet and brush. Freddy behind us vacuuming and drying. It was crazy how we got away with that.

Mother Passes Away

Whilst I was working at Probert Club, I received a message to say my mother was no more. It was very disturbing. My mother had been sick for quite a while and she had been living in hospital. When the news came of her passing away, I was devastated. My father had passed away a few years back and we were now orphans, that was a terrible thing to be. After my mom was buried, we returned to the Hustle again. My mother was a soldier, she taught me to stand all the time like a man. But one other thing she taught me was to trust in our Lord God. No matter what I do I still have faith in our Lord God. Without God I would be lost for good. I do not want to talk about my mother as I get emotional, she was a strong woman.

Clubbing

I was introduced gradually to clubbing by my friend, who I met at the Probert Club. He was a good dancer. I still got some of his moves in me. He taught me to get a little bit naughty and gangster. He was a flirt and used to sleep with hookers which I didn't, he used to take me into pubs looking for hookers. Each time he got really high he would be unstoppable. He would want to sleep with someone. I called him 'Danger'. I suspected from my own diagnosis that he had AIDS, I am not sure but somehow, he resembled someone who had the disease. I wondered why those hookers slept with him, so I called him Danger. That is the same reason I did not want to sleep around with hookers. I only slept with this girl that I found in the club one day, but she was not a hooker. Danger tried to convince me she was as a way of trying to get me hooked to sleeping with hookers but I did not ever try that again. It was a one-night stand and I lied my name. I said my name was James. I remember walking in brothels in Chisipite Avenue in Harare where people would get sex. I was asked if I wanted any, and I refused, but Danger received his treatment from a hooker. I was surprised to see a lot of hookers in a big room selling sex that was the last time I went to that place. There were so many clubs we went to in Harare. The two clubs that we went to were a club called Nerds and the other called Stripping. The clubs were downtown Harare and were frequented by young people because of the type of music they played; which was hip-hop, R&B and Dancehall music. Most of the dressing was American hip-hop gangster style. These were the clubs that we frequented to try and drink away the problems we were facing in real life. The music was so loud I didn't know how I survived from getting deaf. The parties were sometimes very wild, I remember when a song called, 'The Boom', by Sean John and DMX Paul was played, each time all the girls would run away from the dance floor as the boys would start to dance in a very wild way, up and down and sideways, it was mad like a wild bull. Many of the youngsters who went there were very connected and some were from very rich families like government ministers etc. Each time I went there, the cigarette smoke would not come off from my clothes even when I got home, that's how bad it was. Nerds was an underground club in the middle of the city and Striping was on the first floor of a building in the city, both clubs had bouncers who manned the door and searched everyone as they came in. At one point, someone smuggled a teargas canister inside and let it out and there was a stampede to get out of the club. If they did not do that some kids could bring guns because the atmosphere was so tense.

Gradually, I had become addicted to alcohol that one day after I had married Juliet, we were having a party at my friend's house called Thomas. He brought Russian Tsar, a strong stuff equivalent to vodka, and I finished the bottle dry. The last thing I remember was, I was trying to dance to my favourite tune on the radio playing in the house and I passed out. I woke up the following morning with my head aching and drowsy. I had puked all over myself, it was a mess. I had left my house the day before with the intention of going back after the party and my wife came looking for me, I felt stupid. That was crazy I would never try that again. We had one of the wild parties again with my friends where a lot of my friends passed out, those days were crazy.

Working For Eagle Private Investigators

At One time, after I left Probert's Club, I got a job with a company called Eagle Private Investigators. The job involved with collecting money from people who had defaulted from their creditors, it involved tracing them and collecting. I remember being given a job to collect a debt from a failed local radio station called 4FM. I cannot still remember how I did it but I tracked down the owner of the radio station in Harare. It seemed I knew all the corners and could easily track anyone. When I confronted him, he was on the verge of breaking down from debts. He was a dreadlocked guy and had a smart appearance. I shocked him, how I had found him. He told me that he had no money and that he was so broke I felt sorry for him, the man was literally begging me to give him time. I hardly got any money from this business, so I left it.

As time went on, after I was sacked from Probert Club, I started going to internet cafes around town and searching for any prospect on the internet. Internet cafes in those days were used by a few and the elite and foreigners, who were communicating with their relatives back home. As I had worked with a few whites so I knew about them; whilst I was there, I came across a political party which is the opposition party of Zimbabwe known as FDM. The leader of the FDM is known as Richard Mutamiri. They were communicating with their supporters through the internet. I started following them. For the first time, I was angry and I started having an interest in opposition politics. The first person I had met earlier known in Zimbabwe as Katsande, a guy who did soap adverts on Zim-TV had approached me and tried to get me joined to his political party but nothing worked, I think it was just an idea which did not materialise. I started sending encouragement messages to a lady called Nyarai at FDM. After a while, Nyarai send an email to me with details about volunteers

who were required to work in the FDM office. I responded and

Nyarai asked me to come to their offices in Harare. It was called

the FDM Support Centre.

Working For The FDM

After being rejected to work as a volunteer by FDM officials, they told me to start working in my constituency first. I went to my constituency in Seke but honourable Sithole who was the FDM Shadow MP was not taking any new volunteers. After a short while, Nyarai advertised the jobs again for volunteers and I went back again to the offices at their office but this time they really needed someone to start helping as soon as possible. I was engaged with Julia Roberts who was the spin doctor of the FDM in the information department. I soon started to work very hard. The people in the offices were really scared of the ruling UDI agents and it was visible on their faces. I was not moved at all, as I was hardened by the streets. To me, it was a game I needed to play wisely. I knew the risks and I knew what and not to do, violence was not my style I wanted to fight whilst working in administration. That way I fought smart. As time went on everyone started trusting me. They saw the hard work that I put in and the dedication and I started to get recognised. Initially, I was not being paid then someone introduced me to Mr Sean who was the fundraising coordinate in FDM. He understood my situation and he started paying me for working at the FDM. During elections in the year 1999 in Zimbabwe, I was put in charge of the data input department. I was given the keys to the offices as well which means I was the one who opened the offices in the morning and after work closed the doors of the offices by a lady called Lisa. She also gave me a mobile phone. I was in charge of all the monitoring reports that came from polling agents at polling stations. We were capturing all the data regarding how fair the election was. I was in charge of all volunteers mostly white who had come to help with data capture. I also compiled all reports from election observers from all over the world and made it into a booklet which we sent to the legal resources' foundation for safekeeping in Zimbabwe. It was funny and serious business capturing the data. One polling agent, who I think was not very educated, wrote in one of the monitoring form something like 'The erection was free and fair', we all joked about it, that's how we coped in such a tense environment we joked and that took our minds off from the tense atmosphere and got everyone to relax. There were at times tensions between the staff and at times were diffused but one thing I remember was some of the FDM staff from the security who thought the whites were taking over and this resulted in the white volunteers being stopped from coming to the offices as tensions were rising because of that. FDM was now being perceived as a white dominated opposition party. The head of the information department was the late Percy Nhira. Soon after losing the election in Zimbabwe due to mass vote rigging, the FDM continued to raise these concerns to the international community. The election was marred by violence subjected on political opponents by the ruling UDI party. Most of the international political observers thought the election was not free and fair except the African observers who thought it was. The election was soon to be rerun. FDM had managed to get a fair share of its MPs in parliament of Zimbabwe for the first time in the history of Zimbabwe, after winning seats in most of all the urban cities of Zimbabwe, and UDI won most of the rural Areas.

I was given the responsibility to look after party material, like T-shirts which we sold to party supporters in order to raise money for the party. One day Mr Sean sent me into the streets of

Harare to sell some of the opposition party T-shirts. He wanted me to go into Harare City centre but something prompted me to go to the outskirts where I knew I could sell a lot. I went to Belvedere Shopping Centre in Harare and a lot of T-shirts were bought mainly by whites dining there and a few blacks. Each time a black man came they tried to intimidate me, but I was not phased. I remember a police Santana land rover that came and stopped near me, whilst I was selling the T-shirts. One of the police officers said to me, we have Zinjaro in here and you are going on selling T-shirts for FDM. Zinjaro was a shadow member of parliament for Mufakose who was abducted by police and was assaulted severely on his buttocks which were severely swelled and dark from beating when they showed them on the next morning national newspaper, the national news of Zimbabwe. So, when I met the police, that was the day they beat him so much. When I left Belvedere, I remember at one time, I went through a college where I tried to sell a few and then as I was carrying the satchel containing the T-shirts crossing Mandela road towards our offices, I was all of a sudden surrounded by a passing mob of hundreds of UDI Supporters running, singing and chanting party songs. I was so lucky the T-shirts were in the satchel. I continued to move through them without panic and went to our office, I was so lucky I survived that. It happened twice that I met these mobs running and surrounded, each time I was neither touched nor hurt. Our FDM party offices were always under siege from UDI government agents, they used to harass us and some of them were the people I used to see when I was unemployed working for Vital, struggling in the streets. I do not know up to now how they ended up working as intelligent officers for UDI, they had intelligence agency's IDs, and some of them thought we were privileged to work for FDM, I was confused. Sometimes they would say something like if you knew what UDI was doing to you, you would stop going to FDM offices. They said we know what you do, eat, drink, sleep, friends and everything. I became very cautious. Those days I was working with my friend Brian, and many other people employed by the FDM. Lots of MPs used to come to our offices and I was in charge of getting information to them in parliament, I also used to send press releases to the local newspapers from FDM. I remember the day when I was selling T-shirts in Belvedere, I came across a group of touts at Russell hospital bus stop who saw me selling the FDM T-shirts and there was this scary looking stalky tout who came to me and he grabbed my satchel full of T-shirts and was saying,

"These T-shirts belong to us, you cannot sell them". I quickly grabbed the satchel and whispered, you are under surveillance, and he quickly let go the satchel with sudden fear of reprisals. I was so lucky that day I got away with that, unscathed, that was scary. Those guys were notorious, and they were known to beat up people or strip naked women in miniskirts, I was so lucky I got away.

I remember one day, all the security staff of FDM was arrested and Maud, one of the top legislators in the FDM asked me and to look for them at the Harare Southern Police Station. I took a guy who worked for FDM called Mao and we went to the police station. On our way to there, we met an officer called Ruben who used to date my sister and worked in the law and order department of the police at Southern Police Station in Harare. I told him that I was looking for our security staff that had been taken by police and he told me to go and check in his office. He told me they were with another fellow police officer known as Stephen. I said thank you and we went to the police station. We did not stop at reception; we went straight inside the station to Ruben's office. We knocked the door and Stephen opened the door for us and we went inside. We were surprised to see all the FDM security staff in the office and they all looked troubled and one of the security recognised me and everyone was confused including Stephen, but nobody asked why I was there and I told Stephen I just wanted to see these guys meaning the FDM security staff then I thanked and left the building. I went and reported the security staff whereabouts to the staff at FDM and they were released soon after by FDM lawyers' intervention. Maud was assaulted heavily. After I left Zimbabwe, many things happened, we lost the minister of information in the FDM, the department I worked in. He was set up and he committed suicide in prison after he killed his wife, for adultery. The president of FDM was assaulted and many other people lost their lives during the time that I left Zimbabwe, many members were set up by the government and killed or arrested. I considered myself lucky to have left Zimbabwe, but my luck ran out as I will explain in the next chapter *My Journey in Exile in the UK*.

I remember when I worked for the FDM, I used to produce flyers with propaganda for the party using Risograph copiers. I produced loads of flyers a day and I went to Chiredzi with one of the two members of the opposition and his wife to train people in Chiredzi, a town in rural Zimbabwe to use one of the Risograph machines that had been bought for them. I was treated good in

Chiredzi where I slept in a hotel called Greenwood. I was treated like a VIP with the youth in Chiredzi for the FDM. I was shown around the town.

When I left FDM to come to the UK, I had a reference done by the then secretary general of the FDM, Witness Chehore and another by Colin, one of the party officials responsible for our department. In FDM, I worked closely with all directorates which included the elections directorate, international relations and information directorate.

Escape To The UK

n November 2001, on a second encounter to try and get to UK after the first encounter being a failure, where I used my brother's passport as mine was ruined in my first attempt. I managed to get into UK as my brother had used it to come over here before. I was lucky. I started working illegally and the jobs were nasty, people ill-treated me at work and sometimes called monkey and colleagues drop boxes on me whilst offloading boxes in trucks, and I was not being paid for all the hard work by the agency that employed us. It was nasty and we could just get fired anytime and we couldn't do anything to protect ourselves. I also worked for another security company called TTR and the drivers for this company were very crazy, they used to race us to work and sometimes it was very dangerous, another driver had to hit a lamppost onetime because of travelling at excessive speeds that was scary considering he was coming to pick us for end of shift. Another Asian driver was just a nasty piece of work. He was called Harry and he enjoyed driving at excessive speeds and did not care, he smoked weed and at one time he took me to a place where he started dealing in Birmingham, that was before the SIA Badges were introduced, he was nasty and if at all you wanted to get picked and he couldn't do it he would answer like "I don't care, I don't give a fuck." His teeth were all coated with cigarette smoke and looked nasty, one day he took me to his hood in Erdington, where he showed me around and graffiti with his name on it, he told me he was responsible for it. I started making attempts to start making amends to get legal but I only managed that after I had brought my family from Zimbabwe. I was separated from my wife for nearly 10 months and that was torture. There were temptations here and there, but I stayed without any encounter with a woman until my family came from Zimbabwe, who were my wife Juliet and daughter. I loved my family. We had problem here and there but we remained together until I was fed up by problems that we faced and I took off to stay with two boys I had met from work. My sister in law had come from Bianga, Zimbabwe. Life was getting unbearable as the stress levels were high on me due to family problems. I went to stay with Edward and Sam. We enjoyed our time together and thought I had moved on when things took a twist and all of a sudden, the boys were on to me persecuting me. I moved to my new house in hillside and reunited with wife and family but things were just starting to get nastier. At work, I was being bullied and at home the same. I started having a mental breakdown, hating everyone and I chased my wife away from home. She went to live with relatives. The things which were happening are hard to explain. It felt like marital collapse and that scarred me and tortured me. I suspected all sorts. Maybe I was getting crazy. I ended up in a mental hospital with my daughter taken and me being charged with all sorts of things. I knew I was innocent but I was under attack and did not know what was happening. Year 2004-5, I was going through courts, curfews and living alone scared. It was war, the kind of war I had never seen before and I was losing bad, losing my lively hood, losing my family and losing in life. I was being driven to suicide. Started hearing voices and I only recovered in a nasty place, a psychiatric hospital. I was sectioned and was not free to go out. I was mixed with people who were mentally ill. I laughed at myself, what going on I asked. My world suddenly turned upside down. *'This is not what I left Zimbabwe for'*, I thought. But what I wanted to do was to survive. I was asked to co-operate by this black African support worker, and that's what I did until the day they released me in 2006. After being released, I went to be together with my family again and by that time they had tried to move on, that was hurtful. When we moved together initially there was opposition and more confusion, I asked myself what's going on. We managed to have a good wedding with my wife and it was attended by more than 300 people. We lived happily until things started to get nasty again, the system was fighting me, never wanting to let me go. I was receiving injections now and again for mental health problems, and I was in denial, we had our second child, Chenai, I vowed to take my life back and fought hard through getting into University for studying business and computers. I graduated in November 2010 with a 2:1 in Business Management from the University of Worm Bridge. The journey was tough, I had to balance work, study and family. I also had my first driving licence. In a matter of four years; I had a wedding, degree, computer qualification, driving licence all key stones to my life and a two-bedroom house we rented from council which we could call our own, that was an accomplishment. I had completely stopped drinking all together.

During my study period, I was working for P2P Bridge. That was scary and a nasty place to work. The supervisors treated us like dirt and were over worked with little pay, but I enjoyed working there. I just like the experience that I got from working as a cook there.

After graduating, I got a job working for Bisbee City Council on an internship program. This job introduced me to working in government as a civil servant. I was so lucky. My confidence improved. The year was 2011. I went through a very rigorous interview and my job was to be a SME secretariat and working as an enterprise officer. That was my dream job. *'I had made it'*, thought.

I was attending round table board meetings with local black businessmen and women. I was in charge of administering grants working with businesses in Brisbee City Council. The grants I was managing came as a result of riots in 2011; that left most of the shops damaged and I was in charge of giving out grants to those businesses to put security measures in place to protect their businesses and the Mayor was invited to go round and inspect the work done by those grants which was a good achievement for me. I managed to unite black businesses to work together in a network called Brame Club. I acted as the secretariat and used to organise and write minutes for the forum. I got a lot of help from my manager Dinesh Singh and other fellow colleagues at the council. My job broadened my horizons of working in business and I left the council to form my own business called Vital Bits. When I set the business up, I was helped by Christian Evans with office address and temporary offices or virtual office and Norman Vine, the Chair of the Brame Club acted as my mentor and I met both of them through Brame Club. I am now an entrepreneur. I bought my equipment from Brixton, from a guy called Scott, who I had met online, and he also trained me. My wife helped with a £1000 to buy a van and other set up fees I got them from a government initiative to help jobless people start their own businesses, called new enterprise allowance of £1000. With that amount I started my own Vital Bits business.

Alongside this, I was also going to church which my wife belonged to, The Reformed Church from Zimbabwe. I was baptised and was made to join the men's fellowship club. I was then entrusted to be the church secretary and auditor and a lot more jobs that I did to help the church for two years. After my term expired, I gave up the roles to new other people and I started concentrating on my business. This time my business had grown a bit and was hiring many different people to help me, but competition began to grow, and I got lucky to get a contract to supply products for my business from a large organisation. My business has now grown and recently; from humble beginnings to be an entrepreneur and boss. The journey had been tough but worth the while. I have big plans to franchise the business worldwide like what KFC does.

Despite everything that had happened in my life, I still love life and have no regrets. This memoir is meant for anyone who has had or could learn from my struggles in life. Live positively knowing that life is not a garden of roses and despite all that happens in life hold on, persevere and you can make it in your pursuit for happiness.

About The Author

The author is a very bright and intelligent streetwise author, and an avid reader who grew up in Harare, Zimbabwe. He has worked with numerous people from different backgrounds including politicians and journalists and is well connected internationally and at home in Africa.